All about Us

Geraldine Kyles

This is a work of non-fiction; however, some names and facts have been altered for the simple purpose of protecting identities.

Published by CLF Publishing, LLC. 3281 E. Guasti Road Seventh Floor Ontario, CA 91761. (760) 669-8149.

Copyright © 2012 by Geraldine Kyles. All rights reserved. No portion of this book may be reproduced, stored in a retrieval system, or transmitted by any form or any means electronically, photocopied, recorded, or any other except for brief quotations in printed reviews, without the prior permission of the publisher.

ISBN # 978-0-9857372-6-9

Illustrations drawn by Nic Harrison. Contact information is nwharrison@hotmail.com.

Cover created by Senir Design. For information, contact info@senirdesign.com.

Printed in the United States of America.

DEDICATIONS

This book is dedicated to my daughters Angelierdevontae and Antelita, my granddaughter Jour'dan Alana, my deceased parents Emma and Emmett, and my deceased grandmother Nettie.

Angelierdevontae reminded me on a consistent basis about my gift and talent of writing. She would say, "You need to put something in writing."

Antelita reminded me of the 1996 prophecy given to me about writing books. She challenged me to complete what I had begun in 1991.

Jour'dan Alana inspired me to write after seeing her passion for reading.

My parents Emma and Emmett and my grandmother Nettie kept me grounded by being living examples, by each demonstrating a compassionate spirit through words and deeds for mankind without hesitation and without being judgmental.

ACKNOWLEDGEMENTS

Special thanks to

Pastor Mary Logan of Tulsa, Oklahoma, who confirmed my intention and desire to write this book through prophecy in 1996.

Dr. Cassundra White-Elliott, my publisher, for her patience and effort to get me started in making my story heard in book form.

TABLE OF CONTENTS

About Us   7

Our Town   15

Living Apart   29

Can't Stop Now   37

One Big Happy Family   51

A Note from the Author

As a child growing up in the South, I observed and heard many conversations that yet remain with me today. There were many emotional, depressed and suppressed conditions of people all around in my community and other communities.

When I visited other small cities in other states, I detected that most of the people did not enjoy their lifestyle, but they had no idea how to improve or change their poverty mentality. In other words, suffering and living below the poverty level had become a part of them and was just a way of life.

As I was sitting at my table, my mind reflected back to when I had observed several senior citizens, who couldn't read, write or count, being cheated out of their monies by one of the community storeowners. That disturbed me!

As I sat reflecting, I also recalled when my grandmother's sister, who lived in another state, had several acres of land stolen from her as a result of marking an 'X' on a piece of paper just to get a block of cheese, a loaf of bread, and bologna, which they called staples, on credit.

I remember it as if it happened today when I went to the courthouse with my mother to get her mother's sister's acres of land redeemed back to her through the court system. To hear the judge say that the statute of limitations had expired was tragic and the disappointed look on my mother's face was indescribable.

All about Us

About Us

"About Us" is about a group of Southerners who routinely engaged in the same activities on a daily basis. They believed that their way of living was a part of life.

Growing up in the South can be very interesting. You have the Ma and Pa stores, dirt bumpy roads, old disgusting red clay roads, and a host of retired men sitting under a tree playing dominoes, checkers, and shooting the breeze. Would you believe that those old men are under that tree from sun up to sun down?

Every once and awhile, Mr. Bo will pull out a jar of his favorite molasses syrup water and swallow down a big gulp. I can't forget about his old cigar pipe; boy, does it stink. Every day, Mrs. Rosa yells to him, "Put that out! You're gonna mess around and burn the whole town down and make somebody sick." Mr. Bo just grunts and keeps on puffing that old stinky pipe. Then, Mrs. Rosa yells out, "It's nothing like a stubborn old man."

Then, there's Mr. Joe. He has a big pot belly and often wears overalls, a red checkered shirt and big worn out work boots as if he is going to work. Mind you now, he is retired. My mom says when some people have worked so long, they have a tough time getting work out of their system.

Oh! I have got to tell you about Mr. Sam. He wobbles out of his door every morning with a cup of coffee, a plate full of sausage, bacon, eggs, and grits. You know he had to have biscuits on his plate, too. Do you know that he refuses to talk to anyone until the plate is cleaned? My brother and I have him down pat. After Mr. Sam finishes eating, he rubs his stomach, belches, pats his feet, and says, "Man, wasn't that good."

I can't leave out Mrs. Lucille. There is a "Mrs. Lucille" in every town. Now, she is the queen of gossipers. She is the one who keeps the whole town in an uproar. She is in everybody's business. Even her husband gets up and leaves when she comes around. My aunt Kaye says she needs a bridle over her mouth; whatever that is! My dad often says that it's a waste of money to buy newspapers having someone like Mrs. Lucille in your town.

Then, we have Mrs. Geneva. She is just as wild as a jack rabbit. That woman loves to dance. She is known as the 'wild woman on Fruit Road. Do you know that she has the nerve to tell everybody that she is going to be on the show, "So You Think You Can Dance?" She claims to be our town's celebrity. Her husband Mr. Daniel seems to think so, too. After all, they have been married for at least twenty years. He also thinks that she needs to be on "Dancing with the Stars." Like my grandma used to say,

"It's a lazy dog that don't bark some times."

I must tell you about Mrs. Sylvia. If she has her way, everybody in town will look like Mr. Sam, her husband. He is the one who wobbles out of the door. Boy, can that woman cook! You can smell her food a block away. My mother thinks that she intentionally opens the doors and pushes up the windows, so everybody can get a swift. Now, that's cruel! Don't you think?

You must hear about our mailman Mr. Frank. He has been the town's mailman before I was born. Of course, he is up in age. Guess what? That man puts everyone's mail in everyone else's mailbox. We love him so much, so we don't make a fuss. I know that makes him very happy. Jobs are jobs now. Our town gossiper says that most of the time she catches him sleeping in his car. Guess what? She had the nerve to tell *us* not to say a word about it. My grandpa says she couldn't keep a secret if her life depended on it.

Let me tell you about Mrs. Sarah. She is the church lady. She is the one who walks around with those long dresses, bonnet on top of her head and the bible under her arm. She knows how to preach that Word. Let her tell it, everybody is going down if they don't live right and love each other. One thing I can say, she loves people and is always ready to lend a helping hand. My grandma says that's good.

You must hear about the flower lady. Mrs. Audra is a tough nut to crack. She thinks everybody's front yard has to look like hers. Do you know that you can hardly walk in her yard without stumbling over her flowers? I would hate to leave out of her yard during power failure. We try to wait until we think she is cooking or doing the laundry because if she sees us, she tries to push some of those flowers off on us. She is a nice lady, but she needs some wisdom.

Mr. Tony is our seed man. Our town folk plant most of their own crops. He plants everything in his garden and invites the neighborhood to get as much as they want without charge. He is really down to earth.

Now, we have Mrs. Joyce. She really knows how to work a general store. She opens early and closes very late. She makes your heart melt when you walk through the door. She is always in high spirits, full of smiles, and extremely helpful. Let me give you just a little advice: Don't go there when you are pushed for time. She is lonely and loves to converse with everyone. Her children live far away and her husband Mr. Ed died last year. She tells everybody that the store gives her something to do. I can truly say she is a precious little lady.

We have Mr. Carter. He is our town's auto mechanic. Everybody loves him. That man is never unhappy. He says helping people brings him joy, and if he didn't get a dime for his labor, he would continue to do the work. He tells people that this world needs love, and that it's the only thing that is going to turn hate around.

I can't leave out our town's minister, Reverend Young. What a kind man. He blesses everybody, including the birds and the dogs. He always has a kind word to say and is just as humble as pie. My dad says that he's a great man.

I can't leave out our teacher Mrs. Pat. She is tough as nails. I can picture her standing behind that beat up desk wearing the ugliest glasses you ever want to see, for another thirty years. She feels that everyone should be teachers. I know if she hadn't inspired me, I probably wouldn't have made teaching college my career.

I have to introduce our one and only sheriff. Sheriff Jones walks around with a billy club and an old big rusty outdated-looking gun. My uncle Pop says that gun wouldn't shoot if he tried. Everybody loves him.

All about Us

Our Town

"Our Town" was inspired after visiting my grandmother's family during the summer. I recall so vividly the tall, black telephone with a dial almost at the bottom of it. I remember picking up the telephone receiver and hearing two ladies talking.

My grandmother's sister explained that they had two and three party lines. In other words, whenever the phone rang, it was not always for you. My grandmother's sister had a straight ring. Her neighbor had a short ring, and the other neighbor had some other ring.

The town was something out of the ordinary. But, at the same time, it was very unique, and the people were fascinating.

Living in a small southern town can be nice, and at the same time, it can be a little creepy. Everybody knows each other and each other's business.

In our town, we still have that three-party telephone line with the small tall, black telephone that you have to dial. That tells you just how small our town is.

Guess what! We have one general department store where everybody shops, one gasoline station, a Ma-and-Pa store, and auto mechanic shop. You sure guessed it! All of them are owned by Mr. Jones. What a rip off!

I forgot to tell you about our mail. We still have the mailbox with the red flap on the side. The mailman comes three times a week. I guess we are not important! We have had the same mailman since before I was born. Now, in the big town, they deliver mail six days a week. That's cruel!

We do have an elementary school. The school bus takes the older children to the big school. That's in another town! Mrs. Shirley, our next door neighbor, says, "We are living in the dark ages."

Well, maybe she is right! Mrs. Mae, our librarian, feels that someone needs to do something about these party telephone lines.

There is no need to have each other over as a house guest and for parties. You can just pick up the telephone, and you talk to whomever you want. Mrs. Mary is the gossiper in our town. My mom says, "She stays up half the night snooping." She was the one that told everybody in town that Mr. Pete and Mrs. Sue were getting a divorce. My dad says, "She is the Rona Barrett in our town." The sad part about this is she doesn't get paid for it. I guess some people are just born to be nosy.

Mrs. Mamie and Mrs. Sally had a cat fight. Mrs. Sally accused Mrs. Mamie of trying to dress like her. Did anyone get it! We only have one general department store. What a great example for us kids!

On yesterday, we had a new family move into town. I wonder if they checked us out. I heard my mom say that they were from a big place called New York. I found out that they have five children. That's two less than Mrs. Lizzie and Mr. Paul.

Well, our town is getting crowded! Maybe, I'll have someone to play with. You see, I have two older sisters, Kelly and June. They all go to the big school.

By the way, I spotted our new neighbors. They are

pretty cool. They waved to me over their fence. My mom said they came over to our house to introduce themselves while I was at school. Their last name is McCoy.

Mr. McCoy is a computer analyst. Whatever that is! Mrs. McCoy is a teacher. The reason they moved to our small southern town was because they were tired of that big city. They wanted to raise their children in a less congested city. I don't know about us being a city. I guess that's what those sophisticated folk from big places say. Wow! I'm glad they chose us. We can sure use some intelligence around here.

I found out that their twins Emily and Emmett are my age. We will be going to the same school and will have the same teacher. I'm sure excited about that! We can walk to and from school together and maybe spend some time playing together. I do have a lot of toys. Well, most of them my dad and Grandpa Willie made. People in our small town don't like to spend money unnecessarily. They always talk about saving for a rainy day. They sure should have a lot of money because it doesn't rain here an awful lot.

I like when Christmas comes. They go out of their way to make us happy. Do you know last year, I got a big brand spanking new bike? It was red too! I tell you I rode that bike up and down the road. I know in the big cities, they call them streets. Not here! I hear the McCoy children calling our roads streets. They sure have a lot of fancy words. Maybe, some of that can rub off on me. I guess I have to be little more patient.

I heard that the McCoys are planning on getting us some help in this town. They plan to talk to the City Planning Committee. Whatever that is! I found out that they were talking to Ma Bell to get our individual telephone lines and the mayor to get our own post office.

Get this! I even heard that they were bringing in some big time developers to talk about building us a shopping mall.

Wow, that's wonderful! That will mean that Mrs. Mamie and Mrs. Sally won't be cat fighting over clothes.

Mrs. Mae our librarian will not have to walk three miles to catch the bus to the big school because the McCoys have challenged the mayor to get our own library.

Now, check this out! The McCoys are also talking to the mayor to get our own big school. That will be fantastic! These McCoys are a true blessing! I knew that there are some good people in this world. My grandpa Willie used to say, "It's all in God's timing. How true that is!"

Would you believe that some other families caught wind of what's going on in our town? Now, we have three new families moving here.

I wondered why I saw those carpenters working from sun up to sun down. They were building those new homes. How cool!

The McCoys are having a meeting with everybody in our town before they meet with the City Planning Committee and the mayor. They want to know everybody's opinion about improving our town. Can you believe they wanted the children's opinion, too? Wow, how cool!

Well, we had the meeting. Everybody voiced his/her opinion. They pretty much said the same thing. The new families were there. They had a lot to say!

I found out that the Thompsons were from Los Angeles, California, and they have four children. The Youngs have ten children, and they are from Pensacola, Florida, and the Fountains have three children and moved from Chicago, Illinois.

Can you imagine that all the children are pretty much

the same age as the children already living in our town? That's neat!

We are meeting with the mayor and the City Planning Committee on Wednesday at 4:00pm. I am getting nervous! My mom said I have nothing to worry about and to just say what's in my heart. Well, that's easy for her to say because she is a grownup.

The meeting went great! The mayor agreed to sit down with the City Planning Committee and discuss our concerns and needs. He also planned to talk to some outside investors to assist us with the building and improving our town. He told us to give him and the City Planning Committee ninety days, and he will get back with us.

The mayor was impressed with the children speaking. He said, "I have never had a meeting where children spoke and did so well."

He told me that I was going to be a politician. My mom says because I did so well. That's good news!

Well, our new neighbors have all moved into their homes. But the good news is that the mayor and the City Planning Committee came through. We have our new mall, post office, library, big school, another gasoline station, auto mechanic shop, and the biggest of them all- private telephone lines. They even threw in a skating rink and bowling alley. The mayor says he was talking to some developers that have an interest in building us a movie theater. Isn't that real cool? What can I say about all of this? It took one family to get the ball rolling.

Since we have added to our town, brand new homes are going up everywhere. Mrs. Mary, the town gossiper, said, "There are twelve families moving here, including my granddaughter Mary Kate." Well, I guess she would know. After all, her husband Mr. Dan is on the City Planning Committee.

Now that we have something to do and some places to go, we have two bus lines that run straight through the town. We have people coming from those big towns to shop at the mall.

Mrs. Mae's daughter Shelly got an afternoon job at the mall. My sister Kelly said, "She works in a boutique where they sell clothes." I heard that they pay good money. Knowing Shelly, she is saving most of her money. She used to say that she was going to one of those big colleges out there in California.

She might have to reconsider that because they have a nice college not too far from here. I heard on the news that California's tuition and textbooks cost a lot of money.

You can bet that Mrs. Mae is going to do everything in her power to talk her out of it. Everybody says, "She is stingy." I kind of believe that because she would walk three miles to work and back, rather than drive her car. Mrs. Mary says, "She didn't want to spend her money for gas." I guess she would know. After all, she is the town gossiper, and her husband goes fishing with Mrs. Mae's husband.

By the way, Mr. Pete and Mrs. Sue called off their divorce and have two other children. How cool is that?

Their son Billy Joe is in my class. He is sure tall! Their daughter Virginia is in the same grade as my sister June. I don't know about those two! They have always hung around each other. I believe that they talk about boys. I really think they have their eyes on that Dan. He's the smart one and loves to read. He wants to be a writer.

Everybody calls him a bookworm. He sure acts like one. You'll never see him without a book. Usually, it's in his back pocket if he is not reading it.

The twelve families did move in. Now, we have an

extra twenty-five children in our town, and we are expecting more.

We still see houses going up everywhere. Would you believe that I have begun to call our town a city? I guess hanging around those McCoys is really rubbing off on me.

I forgot to tell you that we have our own fire station and our own police station and newspaper company now. Wow, what a city! Our mayor says, "Building up our city is going to put us on the map." How sweet it is!

The mayor of New York and California heard about our fast-growing city. They came to see it and had a meeting with our mayor. We were told that we made history. They had never heard a city with such growth in that short period of time.

Our mayor said it! We are looking forward to something else spectacular. Our librarian, Mrs. Mae said, "Some big city developer had a meeting with our mayor and the City Planning Committee about building a university in our city." Mrs. Josephine, the city controller said in our city newspaper, "Money is being offered by developers as far as Hawaii."

Can you believe our elementary and our big school are

crowded? Mrs. McCoy says, "We have children coming from other cities to enroll in our schools, and there is a long waiting list." Did you know they have to fill out a permit to transfer? Yes, that's right!

I heard my mom telling my dad that some teachers came in from some big states to apply for teaching positions. Well, that is really good news! Mrs. McCoy's sister is visiting her from New York. We found out that she is also a teacher.

Mrs. Mary, the gossiper said, "She is interested in teaching in one of the schools." Well, don't ask me how she knows. After all, her husband is on the City Planning Committee and gets first-hand information.

I learned on yesterday that some people came here to look at our city. They are thinking about retiring here. Well, you know where that came from. You guessed it, Mrs. Mary!

Our mayor said, "For the first time, I am enjoying being mayor." I guess it had to take the McCoys to move here from New York to give him and all of us that extra boost. I can imagine how he feels. Everybody likes to see progress although it might come from others' encouragement.

I'm so excited about our city. Yes, I did say city! I told you that the McCoys have rubbed off on me. After all, they are intelligent.

My grandpa says, "Thank God for the McCoys."

All about Us

Living Apart

"Living Apart" is about a young couple who were married fresh out of high school and started a family two years into their marriage at age nineteen. They had problems communicating and were miserable being in each other's presence.

My mom Betty, my dad Joe and I live in a small town in Texas. My dad left for work one morning and never returned home to live.

As long as I can remember, my dad and mom have argued on a daily basis. I believe that they are one of those couples who love each other but don't know how to express it. I found out that some people are better off living apart.

My dad and mom got married straight out of high school. I was born two years into the marriage. My mom never had a job outside of the home. We had everything we needed in a material way, and for the most part, everything that we desired.

As I reflect, my dad would rather be outside working in the yard when he was home than to be inside of the house with my mom. For some reason, my mom was an unhappy woman and was never satisfied.

I recalled my dad bringing home some roses for Valentine's Day. He handed the roses over to my mom and said, "Happy Valentine's Day, Betty." My mom looked at him in disbelief and said, "What so good about it?" She placed the flowers on the table and went inside of the bedroom. I guess my dad was so used to being rejected and unhappy; he shook his head and walked away.

I have never seen my mom smile, even when I am telling jokes. My dad only smiles when he is outside with our neighbor Mr. Patrick peddling around in the yard. They would talk for at least three hours. I remember my dad was cutting grass and another day painting the fence. Each time I looked outside of the window, my dad would have that big grin on his face. I often pondered in my mind what could they talk about that could be so interesting that would take three hours. There were days where night would fall before my dad and Mr. Patrick would end their conversation.

Guess what? When he came in the house, he would grab a newspaper and stretch out in that big old rocking chair that my grandma gave him a few years ago for a birthday present.

My mom stays in the family room sewing clothes or knitting. I seldom see my dad and her in the same room unless we are eating breakfast or dinner. It appears that they are trying to avoid each other. A conversation is out of the question because it gets heated.

I often see my neighbors and my best friend Jay and his

mother and father together. They do a lot of activities inside and outside of the house. Every Friday night is their family bowling night. Jay tried to get me to join them, but I believe that I would have felt so out of place not having my parents with me. I don't know whether our neighbors or my best friend Jay and his family know that I have family issues.

But, sometimes children need someone to confide in. I try to keep it together emotionally when I am around the neighbors and my best friend Jay. But, please believe me, it is extremely hard. Young people should never be under that kind of pressure. I must say that I would rather see my parents living apart than to see them angry and hear arguing constantly. There were times the tension was thick; you could literally cut it with a knife.

Now that my dad is out of the house, my mom and I are participating in a lot of community activities and enjoying every minute of it. She appears to be very happy and cracking all kind of jokes. I noticed that she doesn't spend that much time in the family room sewing or knitting. We even watch television together.

I never figured out how anyone could be so miserable

and snap out of it so quickly without therapy when another person like my dad was no longer living in the same house. But, I guess anything is possible.

I finally learned that being in compromising conditions will keep you emotionally bound unless changes are made.

My dad came around to visit after a year of moving out. He continues to take care of the yard and the maintenance of the house. He has never discontinued taking care of us. We have a great relationship. We spend at least three Saturdays out of the month with each other and talking about life.

My dad explained that sometimes people tend to rush relationships and marriages and not get to know the likes and dislikes of the individual. We tend to think that individuals are mind readers and think that a person should automatically know what he or she needs, wants and thinks. In other words, we fail to communicate.

Would you believe that he and my mom are communicating on the telephone? I caught her laughing on the telephone while talking to my dad. I also learned that it might be a possibility that I will have my family back together again. My dad says, "Your mom and I are taking one day at a time."

This afternoon, the three of us are going out to dinner, and I am not the only one excited.

Geraldine Kyles

All about Us

Can't Stop Now

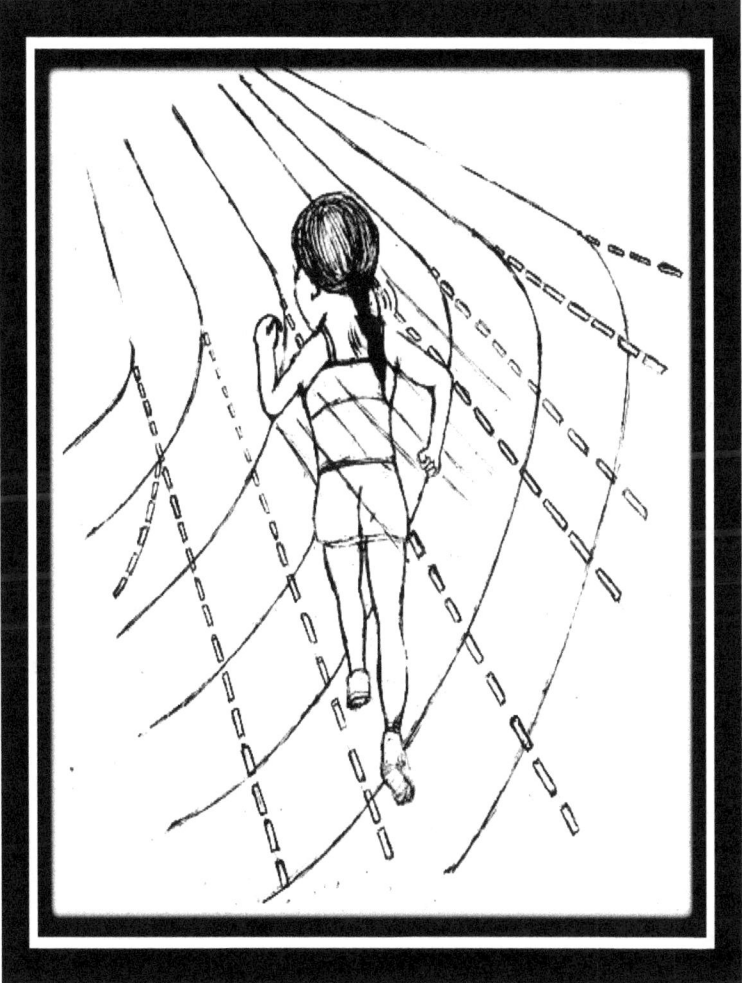

"Can't Stop Now" is about a young girl who vowed to make a change for the people in a southern community.

Many times in school, I have been encouraged to take on different tasks. You see, I love sports; well, not really just sports. I love anything that's mind and body challenging.

You see, I'm from Mississippi. In Mississippi, there isn't a lot to do. People pick cotton, plant crops and sit on the front porch all day long. Some drink moonshine, chew tobacco, dip snuff, hang out under a tree, and pass the moonshine bottle around. Some of them call it shooting the breeze! In Mississippi, we call the tree the stomping ground.

One day, I went to the general store down the street from where we lived. What really got me was old people, like Mrs. Sadie, coming in to get some cheese on credit. Now mind you, Mrs. Sadie couldn't read and Mr. Applegate, the owner, had her to mark an X in a white little book. Before I could leave out the store, there came Mr. Floyd. He wanted to pay his bill. He was another old man that lived in the community. As a matter of fact, he lived around the corner from where I lived.

Mr. Floyd couldn't read or write. Mr. Applegate asked him, "How much you got?" He didn't look in a book or anything. Mr. Floyd couldn't count his money, so he handed it all to Mr. Applegate, which was a fist full. You see, those old people would get a check every first or third of the month. Some would get Mr. Applegate to even cash their check.

As I stood there watching, I actually couldn't believe my eyes.

Mr. Applegate took all of Mr. Floyd's money and gave him fifty cents. Then he had the nerve to ask Mr. Floyd if he was going to get something else on credit.

I made up my mind that day that I was going to do everything humanly possible to get out of Mississippi. You see, I watched those old Black people being taken by some of those White people throughout the years.

They took my aunt Mary's five acres of land. You see, my aunt Mary couldn't read or write. They said, "She didn't pay her bill." Most of the older Blacks never went to school, and some only went as far as third grade. The most work that they did was picking cotton, working on farms, washing and ironing those white folk clothes, and cleaning their houses.

I have watched a lot of young girls have babies out of

wedlock. I know for a fact Mr. Applegate fathered two of Vera's children. Vera was seventeen years old and very pretty. She will slip out of the house at night while her mommy and daddy, Mrs. Lucille and Mr. John were asleep. Everybody in the community knew that Mr. Applegate was messing around with Vera, including her parents and Mr. Applegate's wife. What really blew my mind was nobody said or did anything.

I asked my mother and father why no one did anything about Mr. Applegate messing around with Vera. My mother said, "You need to be quiet and mind your business." Wow, I wasn't expecting to hear that!

My high school physical education teachers Mr. Steen and Mrs. Seabrook saw something in me. They would always put on track and field meets. As a matter of fact, Mr. Steen told me that if I continue to work hard, it would pay off for me.

You see, after thinking about and seeing those old people being taken advantage of, not to leave Vera and those other young ladies out, I made up in my mind that kind of lifestyle was not for me.

I was determined even more to break those cycles that were occurring in Mississippi. I started studying really hard in school and made the honor roll. Every chance I could get, I was running track.

I have received twelve trophies and worked hard with the help of both of my physical education teachers Mr. Steen and Mrs. Seabrook. They suggested that I try out for the Olympics.

I submitted applications to enroll in several colleges. My mother suggested that I enroll in Florida A&M University. She felt that with my honor roll academics and track and field skills I would be a great asset to the university.

This week, I have received admission from seven universities. Two offered me a full scholarship. My goal is to become a counselor and psychiatrist. I will reach back and pull some of the young and old from the trenches that feel that there is no hope, especially in the state of Mississippi.

My goal is to open tutoring schools in every city in Mississippi and Alabama, free of charge.

I'm now attending one of the most prestigious

universities in California. I am on the Dean's list and yet training vigorously in track for the Olympics.

I continue to keep in touch via way of letter and occasionally telephone with my former high school physical education teachers Mr. Steen and Mrs. Seabrook. They are somebody special!

By the way, I talked to my mother. She said, "Vera is expecting another child." Something needs to be done about that! Where is the law when it is needed?

My mother also said, "Mr. Floyd is not doing so well. His feet are swelling." You know, you can't get those old folk in Mississippi to go see a physician. They love to use home remedies!

Well, I have a spring break coming up. I'm trying to decide what to do. I really don't want to go back home to Mississippi. I don't want to deal with all that negativity. It really gets under my skin when I see helpless people being taking advantage of, and there isn't anything I can do about it.

Do you know the sad part about this situation? Those old people think that Mr. Applegate is a good man and just doing them a favor.

I don't know what in the world is wrong with Mr. Applegate's wife. She knows what's going on with Vera and her husband. I found out that her grown children know about this too. When they come in town, they stop to see Vera and the kids. That is mind bothering!

I was told that Mrs. Applegate was afraid to leave him because she has no money or working skills. I can't see her children turning their back on her. But you never know! It has been said that Mr. Applegate helps take care of them, and they don't want to be excluded out of his will.

You know, it seems that people who do wrong live a long time, and the good ones die early. I do know I sure wouldn't miss him!

Well, I decided to stay here in California with my friends. Their mothers invited me to stay with them and go to church.

You won't believe this! I attended a church that is named Love, Peace, and Happiness Christian Fellowship. I enjoyed the fellowship. The people were friendly, and the pastor and his wife were as friendly as the congregation.

The pastor's message was right on time. It was entitled "Nothing Happens Without God Knowing About It."

My goodness, that was refreshing! It let me know that God will deal with wrongdoers.

Now, I know that Mr. Applegate is going be dealt with. I realized more than ever now, you can't do wrong and continue to do wrong and get away with it.

Can you believe I have almost completed a year of college? My grades are very good. I have a four point zero average, and I'm yet on the Dean's List. Next month is my Olympics tryout. My dad and mom plan to attend.

By the way, I talked to my mom this afternoon. She said, "Mr. Applegate's wife finally left him." My dad said, "She got some big-time lawyer from Atlanta, Georgia." He also said, "Mrs. Applegate's lawyer planned to hang him out to dry."

I know that you're not supposed to wish any bad on anyone, but I can't help to say he had it coming. Just think about how many lives that man ruined and all those old folk in Mississippi he has taken advantage of.

Do you know I made the United States Olympic Team? Would you believe Mr. Steen and Mrs. Seabrook were there cheering me on? I guess they told my mom and dad not to tell me they were coming.

That was okay! I kind of like good surprises. However, they made my day.

I could tell that they were extremely proud of me. I truly believe that God put them in my life more than to encourage me, but to also be my shadow.

Well, I brought home a gold and silver. We represented the United States well. I am still feasting over everything that transpired. I met and enjoyed other athletes from the United States and other countries as well.

Can you believe I will be graduating from college next month? How time flies! Guess what? I graduated magna cum laude. My mom said she is bringing a special guest.

Well, the big day is here. Do you know I didn't get any sleep last night? I have longed for this day.

My parents, grandparents on both sides of my family, Mr. Steen, Mrs. Seabrook and their families all attended.

I looked out and saw all had big Kool-Aid grins on their faces. I thank God for knowing such great people.

Well, I know that you have been waiting for me to tell you about the special guest. Let me tease you just a little.

She has four children and is now working on her GED. That's right! It was Vera. My mom said, "She had to get her away from that situation."

Would you believe Vera has completed her first semester in college? She said I inspired her. She wants to be a lawyer!

I plan to further my education. I'm going for my master's this fall. At the same time, I am working on getting the tutoring school started. The federal government is giving me a grant.

I will have my first school opened here in Mississippi by the summer.

I have a long list of students. Guess what? Mr. Floyd and Mrs. Sadie have also signed up.

That's goes to show that you are never too old to learn.

Well, I am on a roll. The federal government has approved another grant. I will be opening up my third school in the spring.

Mr. Floyd and Mrs. Sadie are reading. We got them to open a bank account. Their checks are going straight to the bank.

I heard that Mr. Applegate is highly upset. He's blaming me for Mr. Floyd's and Mrs. Sadie's transformation. I am just not allowing him to steal any more money from those old people.

I caught news that he is even mad about Vera breaking up with him and blaming me for her going to college.
Guess what! It wasn't actually me breaking him and Vera up.

I was told that singing bishop from New Orleans, Louisiana came to Mississippi to run a revival, and Vera got saved. Thank God for him!

Mrs. Applegate's lawyer did just what she said! He did hang Mr. Applegate out to dry. The courts made him sell the house and give Mrs. Applegate half of the money and split the money in his bank account. He was also ordered to pay alimony.

You wouldn't believe that Mrs. Applegate's name was nowhere near that bank account.

They have gone their separate ways. Mrs. Applegate met a professor at Tuskegee Institute College. Oh yes, he's black! And they appeared to be in love.

Mr. Applegate is living in a retirement home and mad at the world. He is yet blaming people for his problems.

Oh, by the way, Vera has completed college and is now practicing law and talking about marrying a lawyer.

Her four children are as cute as buttons and very smart too.

I have my doctorate degree. I am a counselor and a psychiatrist, and I have twenty tutoring schools all over the state of Mississippi and Alabama.

Geraldine Kyles

All about Us

One Big Happy Family

"One Big Happy Family" is about a military husband and father who had to leave his family to fight in the Iraq War.

Every morning, I rush out of bed to hear water running, the smell of coffee brewing, the smell of bacon frying and eggs, and sometimes even over-toasted bread.

With a loud yell mom says, "Breakfast is ready." Why I am not surprised!? Mom is counter clockwise and punctual. Mom is a stickler when it comes to eating breakfast.

My sister Pat and my brother Sam always go to bed thinking about food. I believe that they even dream about it.

Pat says, "1 can't wait 'til morning." Sam says, "Me too." Sometimes, mom has to stop those two from eating so much because we are always late for school.

My grandmother Liz thinks they have tapeworms. Mr. Wade, our school bus driver, used to wait. But because we are always late for the bus, he pulls off and leaves us.

I hate seeing Mrs. Betty, my teacher. She stands at the door and makes the same remarks, "Not again! David, you must get to school on time." I wish she lived with us. She would quickly find out that I'm not the one who's making us late everyday.

I wish my dad was home, but, of course, he can't be here. He is away fighting a war in Iraq, just like my Aunt Jean.

My mom does not tell us much. She says, "Dad will be home soon."

We get letters from Dad. He says, "Somebody has to show patriotism for our country." I guess he is right! I know that he is not the only dad fighting in the war. My friend Mary's dad is there, too. They really love our country!

My best friend Kyle's dad tries to make up the difference because my dad is away. He takes us to the park, little league baseball games, and even to the movies. It's good that someone around here is thoughtful although it's not like having my dad around.

Kyle's dad asked me, Joe, by the way is my middle name, "What would you like to be when you grow up?" I had to really, really think hard. You see, before my dad went to Iraq, I wanted to be a pilot. Oh yes, just like my dad! But, I am thinking that maybe that is not such a good idea. I might have to be away from home fighting in wars like my dad.

I can tell my mom misses my dad very much, but she will never tell. She does not want to make us sad. I can't tell you enough, moms are truly special.

I wonder what my sister Pat, my brother Sam, and I would do without having her around. We try not to give Mom a hard time. We help around the house to lighten the load. We clean our rooms, mow the lawn, water the grass, and even feed our dog, Spotty.

My sister Pat likes to hang around in the kitchen. She even tries to help mom bake cookies. Yesterday, she helped her bake bread.

My brother Sam and I think she likes to hang in the kitchen because she likes to eat, especially cookies.

Today, we got a letter from my aunt Jean. She is the aunt that is in Iraq. Oh yes, just like my dad.

By the way, Aunt Jean is a nurse. My mom told us that Aunt Jean takes care of the sick people in the Iraq war. I am glad that she is able to help. Aunt Jean is my favorite aunt. By the way, she is my dad's older sister. My dad's younger sister Mae lives in Europe. We haven't seen her in three years. Her husband John is also in the military. Come on, I know what you're thinking, a family full of military folk. Is that such a bad idea?

My mom told us that Aunt Jean will be home next month. Wow! That is good news. My grandmother Liz can't wait! Grandmother Liz said that she and my grandpa Bill are going to have a big party the day Aunt Jean gets back in the country from Iraq.

By the way, today we got a telephone call from my dad from Iraq. He is doing fine. He has another three months before he will be home. We can hardly wait. I know my mom feels the same.

Today, my aunt Jean came home from Iraq. My grandmother Liz and my grandpa Bill met her at the airport. My mom, my sister Pat, my brother Sam, and I went to the airport to get my aunt Jean, also. We hugged, kissed, jumped up and down and cried. It was happy occasion!

I wished that you could have seen that big long airplane. Now, I know why my dad loves to fly them.

My aunt Jean said, "It was the smoothest ride." I think I will be a pilot. Aunt Jean was tired and went straight to bed. Tomorrow, my grandmother Liz and Grandpa Bill will give Aunt Jean a 'Welcome Back Home' party. Grandmother Liz has already invited all of her friends and neighbors to the party.

You wouldn't believe who was there. It was my teacher,

Mrs. Betty. I didn't know that Mrs. Betty went to school with my Aunt Jean. What a small world!

It has been two months since my aunt Jean has been home from Iraq. She is still in the military, and she goes to the military base everyday. It is hard to tell whether Aunt Jean liked her stay in Iraq. I see her staring at the ground a lot, and she likes to be by herself a lot, too.

My dad has one more month before he will be home. We can hardly wait. My sister Pat, my brother Sam, and I are marking the calendar.

My mom is being a little more cheerful these days. She is not saying much, but it is written all over her face that she too is counting down the days before Dad will be home. I wonder what my grandmother Liz and Grandpa Bill are going to do when my dad comes home from Iraq. It's hard to tell these days. They are spending a lot of time with my Aunt Jean. But knowing them, they are going to be excited and probably put on a big scene.

Today, we got a letter from my dad. He said that he can't wait to get home to see us. The feeling is mutual! Dad has seven days to go, and he'll be home.

We are yet counting the days. SIX, FIVE, FOUR, THREE, TWO, AND ONE!

Instead of going to school today, we are on our way to the airport to meet my dad. My mom, sister Pat, brother Sam, Grandmother Liz, Grandpa Bill, and Aunt Jean are all excited. None of us got any sleep the night before.

When the airplane landed on the runway, we cheered, jumped up and down because my dad was finally home.

On Saturday, the very next day, there was a party for my dad. There were a lot of dignitaries at the party. Everybody was happy to see my dad and was proud that he served our country well in Iraq.

Guess who else was at the party? Yes, you're right, my teacher, Mrs. Betty. This time, she brought her husband. I heard someone say, "They sure make a nice couple."

My dad's younger sister Aunt Mae wasn't able to come. Her daughter had the chickenpox.

By looking at my dad's face, I could see the happiest man in the world. I was proud to have him as my dad.

My mom was so happy to see all the people showering my dad with all that love. My grandmother Liz was overwhelmed and my grandpa Bill couldn't believe his eyes. I really didn't know that there were so many caring people. I guess you can't underestimate people. My sister Pat and brother Sam were tired. You know they didn't get any sleep the night before. They were curled in a chair fast asleep.

Now, our family is complete. My dad and my aunt Jean have since retired from the military and are working regular jobs. My dad says, "There is a lot of making up to do!"

My aunt Jean is engaged to marry her high school sweetheart, Bobby. What a great guy! The wedding will be next June.

My best friend Kyle and his dad are fine. We still go to the park, little league baseball games, and to the movies together. Guess who joins us now? You got it, my dad!

My grandmother Liz is doing great. She loves to dig in her flower bed. What beautiful flowers she has! They smell good, too.

Grandpa Bill is fine. He goes fishing three times a week. He says, "Fishing is my passion."

My friend Mary's dad is still in Iraq. He really loves his country. He volunteered to fight in the war for another year. What a great man!

Well, I know you are wondering about my mom. She can't be any happier. She and my dad act like newlyweds. As a matter of fact, they are renewing their wedding vows next month.

By the way, my aunt Mae, her husband John, and their daughter Sue will visit us this summer. They are coming to celebrate Grandpa Bill's seventieth birthday.

My sister Pat, my brother Sam, and I are three happy kids. Our family will really, really, really be complete. We are going to enjoy every minute of it!

www.ingramcontent.com/pod-product-compliance
Lightning Source LLC
Chambersburg PA
CBHW060430050426
42449CB00009B/2230